Build That Wall

Devotional Thoughts on Depression

By
Gail Gritts

Introduction

We are going to start visiting on the topic of depression. I try to avoid this topic because I find it very personal, as I experienced a long session of depression and find myself still, at times, having to do battle.

Somehow, I'm no techy and could probably not find it again, but I noticed the demographics for one of the groups where I share my videos. Finding that the larger age groups were those from ages 30-45, I remembered that at that age I experienced my deepest depression.

I had to giggle as I thought about adding Covid19 to the mix of my craziness from that time and how I longed for someone to point me to ideas, solutions, and hope. It is my prayer that this set of devotions and thoughts can be of help to any of you who are suffering.

I'm not putting myself out there as an expert, but just one who has walked the path and found God faithful to take me through, and I'm willing to share with you.

If you look back on my YouTube channel, you will find more on anxiety, fear, and other topics. Or, these video lessons are available in eBooks or paperbacks entitled Light that Shines and Contentment and Captives if you want to read and study more for yourself.

Table of Contents

Build That Wall

Depression sounds like a depressing topic. Sometimes we want to use other words, like anxiety or panic attack, or stress to describe what we are feeling, but I believe many of these are just symptoms a deeper struggle.

When I was struggling with depression, I kept looking for that one key—that one thing that would change me back to what I thought was normal. What I was really doing was looking for a way out instead of the way through.

We will talk about keys and ways to help ourselves more readily, but you must remember that healing from depression is a process. As I've grown, I've come to learn ways to circumvent this aggravation, to see it coming, and even ward it off.

To begin with, let's try defining it. Anyone who has experienced depression will give you a definition based on their experience. A trained counsellor knows depression takes many forms with a wide variety of causes and symptoms. Some indicators are being tired without cause, sad without reason, hungry when you have just eaten, wanting to sleep when you have just gotten out of bed, or wanting to escape when you aren't being pursued.

Some of these indicators are also true for anxiety, stress, and that general feeling of uneasiness. Fears, inability to concentrate or make decisions, forgetfulness, uncontrolled thoughts, and many other things come with depression.

We will cover most of these throughout our visits, but today I want to talk about a couple of Scriptures and a way of thinking God gave me as I began to come out of my depression.

You see, you can't stay there forever. It's not a nice place. God has more for you than perpetual sadness and pity.

So, go with me to Proverbs 16:32, and I want to lay a foundation for our next few visits. The scripture reads, "He that is slow to anger is better than the might; and he that ruleth his spirit than he that taketh a city."

Then, in Proverbs 25:28, we read, "He that hath no rule over his own spirit is like a city that is broken down. and without walls."

We need walls! Walls are protection from the enemy. They give definition, parameters, and location. Without them, the city is vulnerable to attack. This is what God showed me. If I cannot rule my spirit. I am vulnerable. If I allow anger or any other emotion to be the ruler, I am weakened. If I learn to control my emotions, I gain strength.

When I was in the depths of depression, my emotions were in charge. I was up and down, happy and sad, angry and broken-hearted, logical to a fault and completely and irrationally illogical in my responses and demands. I knew I was not making sense, but I felt helpless to rope in my feelings. I could not express them adequately. I was vulnerable to every wind of circumstance and felt like a grey cloud hung over my head consistently.

Here's the weird thing for me. I could lay that all aside and do church, then the minute we drove away, the cloud would appear. I know now it was spiritual warfare, but back then, I thought it was me; that I was inadequate. I was at fault. I was helpless. I had no walls!

I needed that first wall – the wall of perspective. This is the warning wall – the wall that has the drawbridge! The one where you can stop the enemy from entering! The one where the watchman calls out!

First thing – determine the cause. Get perspective.

Why are you feeling like this? Richard Winter, in his book The Roots of Sorrow: Reflections on Depression and Hope says, "Our perspective on what is happening is vital to our sense of hope. So much depression arises because of loss of perspective."

We don't take time to think about what is happening around us before we react by emotion. We see the enemy coming, but we don't pull up the drawbridge. We hear the warning sounding, but we continue going about our business.

Hearing the warning signals is now one of my vital keys. When gloominess appears, I look to see what is going on.

Do I have unpaid bills?
Do I have a to-do list that is haunting me?
Have I lost a few nights of sleep?
Not drank enough water?
Not eaten good food?
Have I unresolved conflict?
Am I afraid to face a problem that needs resolution?
Have I received an unexpected criticism?

Do I have unconfessed sin?
Or even, am I getting too lazy in my personal life, creating guilt and self-accusation?

The list could go on, but if we ignore these things, if we procrastinate, if we shove them aside, they do not go away. They grow and gain ground.

So, the first key is – when you hear a warning signal – do something about it! Pay that bill, seek forgiveness, take care of yourself, forgive others, confess your sin, and ask for God's help.

Every time you do that, you gain back ground, and your wall gets stronger; your warning signals get louder and your drawbridge more secure.

Key number two – admit that you are depressed.

We talked about people trying to hide their anxiety. Go back and listen to the first two videos if hiding is what you are doing. Hiding is a strenuous job! It drives you deeper and deeper. Hiding your depression is the same. It only gives ground to the enemy and will not lead you to the light.

Find a good friend or trusted person and say, "Pray with me please, I'm feeling depressed." Let them ask you questions and help you find the source and then, do something about it.

This is the principle of James 5:16 – "Confess your faults one to another, and pray one for another, that ye may be healed." Confess it – it takes the enemy's power away and gives you hope. When you share it with a trusted friend, you are no longer alone.

So, until we visit again, let's begin with memorizing and meditating on those two verses from Proverbs. 16:32, 25:28.

Start visualizing your life as a walled city. Don't worry right now if there are holes or crumbled walls; we will work through those together. For now, ask the Lord to show you the cause of your feelings of heaviness.

If it is spiritual warfare, if it is pick up your shield!

Charles Spurgeon experienced depression. He wrote, "I like in my times of trouble to find a promise which exactly fits my need, and then to put my finger on it, and say, "Lord, this is thy word; I beseech thee to prove that it is so, by carrying it out in my case. I believe that this is thine own writing; and I pray thee make it good to my faith. I believe in plenary (absolute) inspiration, and I humbly look to the Lord for a plenary fulfilment of every sentence that he has put on record."

If the source of our depression is things you have left undone, get them done – make that call, seek that forgiveness, get things right, clear your plate. "To him that knoweth to do good, and doeth it not, to him it is sin" James 4:17. Procrastination will not move you forward!

And, if you are trying to hide your hurts. Find a trusted friend who will pray with you and be honest with them. "The fervent prayer of a righteous man availeth much" James 5:16.

Tools for Healing

Last visit, we talked about two keys to dealing with depression. 1) listen for warning signals. Look to see what happening around you 2) admit you are depressed. Enlist a prayer warrior. And I challenged you to meditate and memorize two verses from Proverbs and visualizing your life as a walled city. Are you ready to do some work on those walls?

We are going to start by giving you some tools. You can't dig yourself out of depression with your fingers! And you can't build a wall by wishing. You need real and powerful tools. I'm speaking of the tools given by the Creator, Himself. The power of our obedience to God's word!

The first tool I call—Open Exposure.

So, go with me again to James 5:16. "Confess you faults one to another, and pray for one another, that ye may be healed." We need to look more into this tool.

The word fault means a falling aside when one should have stood upright. It indicates a falling away from truth or a false step. Depression is a stepping or falling aside. It is keeping us from standing upright. It a blockage! To move forward, it must be cleared!

Coming face to face with our faults is not a nice thing. We feel humiliated, fearful, and helpless. Our human nature, our heart, does not want to accept responsibility, but this is the key to healing. The wound is ours. The pain is ours. The fault or failure lies within us, and it must be exposed through confession.

Confession is a verbal acknowledgment that there is sin, or fear, or failure that need to be stated and addressed. It is saying more help is needed to solve the issue, and the problem must be laid on the table in no uncertain terms.

Acknowledging is the first step toward spiritual healing and restoration. It also comes with wonderful promise in 1 John 1:9. "If we confess our sins, he is faithful and just to forgive us our sins, and cleanse us from all unrighteousness."

We are not alone in this. The verse exhorts us to find a brother or sister who will take our confession with us to God in prayer. The other person is not a mediator or confessor, but a spiritual, listening ear with the power of prayer. No other person can confess your sins to God for you but yourself, but they can pray for you as you open your heart to God. Their role is to hear, rebuke, correct, instruct, and pray with you and for you.

By now, I hear you saying, "But Gail, I can't believe my depression is due to sin! You aren't being kind and compassionate. You don't understand."

Oh, my dear friend, I do! Initially, you might not see the sin involved in your depression, but I assure you it is there. It isn't for me to point out, but for God to reveal. And, in my experience, He will reveal plenty along the way to healing. Most of us aren't depressed by open, blatant sin; we find depression dwelling in our doubts, our unbelief, our self-focus, anger, unforgiveness, and all sorts of unseen things. That's why healing takes a while! But they need to be exposed! So, don't shut me down yet. There is still hope.

Let me walk you through how to use this tool of Open Exposure.

First, confess – A simple statement of the problem, without excuse or defensive explanation, is best practice. This should be done verbally before the other person. Any explanation should be minimal. A simple, "I am really struggling with _____ (depression), will you pray with me?" Or "I have (committed a known sin) _____, will you pray with me?" That is adequate.

After you have confessed the problem, tell the other person what is resulting. "My _____ (depression) is causing me to_____ (have angry thoughts, feel suicidal, want to hide, think people are talking about me)."

Or, if the problem is a known sin, then say, "I have _____, I know it is wrong, and I need God's forgiveness."

Ideally, you should both go immediately to the Lord in prayer. Following that, the other person might want to share Scriptures or give you some direction or even ask you a few questions for clarity, but the emphasis should be on bringing this before the Lord.

You need three things to make this tool work properly.

First, you need to share with a spiritually mature person who will keep your confidence and be able to give you godly counsel.

You must be acting my faith, trusting that God alone will honor His word and that you stand in a place of blessing by your obedience.

And, there must be prayer – not just a good talking it out, but placing the matter before the Lord with a confident expectance of release and healing.

Why would this matter? Because only your Creator knows you fully! No person can touch your heart as He! His touch is always tender and drawing, even when He has to point out our failures or faults. You need that tender touch – that healing touch that comes from His unconditional love for you.

Following James 5:16 brings release from bondage. It gives you a spiritual confidant and helps you move forward by faith. As you begin seeing God work in your life, confidence grows, and freedom brings liberty.

We've taken a rather long look at James 5:16, but if you are going to wield a tool well, you need to understand its purpose!

I want to show you three more tools in God's toolbox that He used in my life from Revelation 12:11 – "And they overcame him by the blood of the Lamb, and by the word of their testimony; and they loved not their lives unto the death."

To overcome – that's what we want, isn't it? To overcome these feelings, to overcome the enemy? Well, this verse gives us three tools for that purpose.

1) The Blood of the Lamb.

I've never found much teaching on this principle, but when the Lord revealed it to me, I used it anyway! Here's how I see it. As a born-again Christian, I am covered by the blood of Christ. My sins are forgiven. God sees me through the lens of Christ's sacrifice. I stand forgiven. No condemnation. That's what my Bible tells me.

So, when the enemy, or my mind, starts hurling accusations and making me feel worthless, I claim the Blood of Christ. The enemy can say what he wants, my mind can whirl, but that does not change the fact that is settled for all eternity – I am covered by Christ. I am complete in Him. I am loved with an everlasting love. I am His, and He is mine.

I learned to pray this truth. "Dear Lord, I am tempted to believe_____, But your word says, _____, so I ask you to cover me now, and protect my heart and mind by the Blood of Christ."

I would pray for covering protection as I went to bed because it was in dreams and thoughts where the enemy raged. And God protected my mind throughout the night. At times, I still have to pray this prayer.

Why would I start teaching you to build walls from here? Because unless you are building walls built on God's truth, they will crumble! You need a sure foundation under every wall. Only your confession and the Blood of Christ can give you that foundation. Depression is a spiritual battle – and you need spiritual tools!

2) The next tool in this verse is the word of testimony.

    Speak about the Lord. Rehearse to yourself the wonderful things He has done for you. And, speak of Him to others. Tell what you are learning – especially to your prayer partner. Look for things to be thankful for, and tell someone else! Don't keep your spiritual blessings a secret.

3) And, love not your life.

    This is the total opposite of what we are taught today. We spend so much of our Christian life hearing about God's love for us, His acceptance of us, how we need to love ourselves, and that we are worthy and beautiful in His sight – which we are – but that gets our focus too much on self! Love not your life – be willing to sacrifice – give of yourself to others – even to the point of martyrdom. It takes me back to the Job 13:15. "Though he slay me, yet will I trust Him."

    And the example of Job in how God released him when he prayed for his friends.
    So much of the source of depression is self-focus. Be honest, when you feel low, who are you mainly thinking of? Where do your thoughts dwell?

    I found I was constantly thinking about myself – what would make me happy, how mistreated I was, how useless I was, how I would never measure up, how I always failed.

Remember what we said about always and never? Always and never are never always true! They signal a lie lurking in our thinking!

Okay, so you now have four tools – Open Exposure, The Blood of Christ, The word of your testimony, and self-sacrifice.

Next visit, we will look at some more tools straight from God's word to combat direct attacks. These are the bricks that make up the wall as we continue building on this foundation.

Until then, keep meditating on Proverbs 16:32 and 25:28. Keep thinking of your life as a walled city and start using these four tools to prepare your foundation.

The N's of the Night

How are you doing with your foundation? Have you found a trusted person who will pray with you? Are you getting Scripture into your thoughts? Are you working with those tools?

Before we had a whole load more, lets' review. Tool one is James 5:16 – open exposure -confession...finding that person to share and pray with.

Tools 2-4 come from Revelation 12:11 – The blood of Christ, the word of your testimony, and the sacrifice of self.

I want to look at bit more at that fourth one before we can adequately move to looking through the whole tool box.

Love not your life does not mean self-deprivation. It's not a call to self-harming in any form, whether by refusing to eat or cutting yourself or anything like that. God's word never condones self-harm. What this tool promotes is priority – that God should be our first love. That is the first and great commandment, right? – to love God with all our heart, soul, and mind. And then, to love our neighbour as ourselves.

Part of the problem with depression is that this gets out of order. When we are depressed we get over-focused on self. Love for God is more a token, and love for others is second place. I know that is hard to hear, because when you are depressed, you are putting out all the effort within you to appear kind and loving to others, but it seems such a hard thing to do. You get too resentful to give more. Can't they see you are doing all you can? Why do others keep asking more of you? If this is where you are, don't give up, stay with me.

God knows we get things out of order. He knows confusion can set in, and He will help us get this sorted out...in His time. So, don't feel guilty, just trust His word — we must put self into the right place!

Now, I want to take you through something I call the N's of the Night. Once I had victory over my depression, I went back and looked more logically and with less emotion so I could evaluate the thoughts that had plagued my heart and then to look for the biblical response. It even tried to write about them. It's another of my incomplete projects! Maybe someday. But for the purpose of our visits, I want to share some of what I discovered.

Jeremiah 17:9 says the heart is desperately wicked. Psalm 64:6 says the heart is deep. We have to admit that our hearts can surprise us sometimes with things that come out of it. Our minds are subject to our hearts and an amazing number of wild imaginations can plague us. Usually this happens when we are alone, unoccupied, or resting. And especially, when we are depressed or feeling low.

2 Peter 2:7-9 says Lot vexed his soul with the things going on around him. I found that thoughts vexed my soul when I was depressed. And as I studied, I put them all into words that start with N and then all of the biblical responses into words that start with P.

So, the first one I studied was Nonsense. Dreaming can be a natural outlet for the imagination or it can be a haunting place for ridiculous and extreme scenarios. In that partially coherent state of the mind wanders and sometimes the individual is awakened by the nonsensical visions. The imagination can then be judged by the awakened mind as nonsense and be swept aside by reason. Or, the heart may jump up and grab the thought, tempting the individual to entertain the idea a little longer. This will lead to more nonsense and usually the dreamer says, "Oh, how ridiculous" and go back to sleep.

But when the mind is weakened by depression or illness, we are more vulnerable to nonsensical thoughts.

God gave us great potential in our intelligence. We have the potential to invent, learn, explore, and improve, but nonsense is an offense to this gift. When the mind has a steady diet of wasteful thinking, the potential for productivity and healthy living is inhibited.
The wise individual will recognize nonsense for what it is and cast aside those thoughts without remorse. The foolish individual may recognize the nonsense, but prefers to continue the game. He doesn't want to be disciplined or restricted. He views his imaginations as an expression of his character with merit. Herein is the lie. He is only revealing the foolishness of his heart, not the merit of this character.

Others may not recognize the nonsense of their thoughts and are then bound by poor decisions and sad consequences. The heart feeds on what it is fed. If we read, watch, and listen to quantities of nonsense in our waking hours, it is no wonder our heart embellishes those morsels at night. Foolishness is a part of our sinful nature – bound in the heart of a child, Proverbs 22:15.

So, we need a tool! There are loads we can draw on. We can capture that thought and stomp it out. We can ask it those three questions and refuse to entertain it any further, or we can change gears – think about something else.

But before we get to the tool that starts with a P, let's look at a great verse God showed me that helped with these nonsensical thoughts. Proverbs 24:9 – "The thought of foolishness" – look! God knows we think foolishly! The thought of foolishness! The verse goes on to read, "the thought of foolishness is sin."

SIN!!!! That sounds so harsh! But really, God is warning us – foolish thoughts are a warning signal!

Entertaining wild, ridiculous nonsense is a waste of our God-given intellect, a place for the enemy, and a non-healthy, potentially hazardous exercise of no eternal value.

Our tool against these thoughts is found in Philippians 4 – Praiseworthy – if there be any praise the Bible reads – think on these things!

Training the mind to recognize nonsense, to be accountable for thought processes, and to be discerning in what it entertains leads to a healthier thought life.

Discover what is feeding your foolish thoughts and put a stop to it! Just as our physical health is bettered by discipled eating, rest, and exercise, so the mental health is benefitted by discipline in the thought life. What are you watching, reading, and listening to? Are you overtired or malnourished? All these things matter.

Do a Bible study comparing foolish and wise thoughts – a good diet of Proverbs helps here.

Memorize scripture to use as weapons in the night. 1 Cor 13:11 is a good one. "When I was a child, I spake as a child, I understood as a child, I thought as a child; but when I became a man, (mature) I put away childish things."

Exercise self-discipline. When a foolish thought appears, confess it as sin and refuse to dwell on it any longer. Remove yourself from situations or places or people where foolish thoughts are likely to rise.

Seek Christ's aid. Call upon the Holy Spirit to teach you to discern between foolishness and wisdom. And, if you are still haunted with these thoughts, it is time to call upon a spiritual friend and practice open exposure! James 5:16

So, the first N is Nonsense and the biblical tool is thinking on things that are Praiseworthy.
We will have to stop here for today,

But for now, keep meditating and memorizing Scripture, work on your foundation by practicing James 5:16 – Open Exposure – find that trusted friend!

And apply Revelation 12:11 – Let the blood of the Lamb be your covering, speak for Christ, and love not your life – get your loves in the right order. Jesus and Others and You – JOY!

Begin facing down those foolish thoughts by trading them for Praise!

Next visit, we will take on a few more of the N's of the Night and try to un-weave the web of thoughts that cause us such trouble when we are low or depressed.

More N's of the Night

Let's look at a few more N's of the Night. Let's start with Negatives.

"It will never work out, it's useless to try. You can never do that. No one really cares." These, and similar phrases, play over and over in the mind. They hope to sound enough like truth that that we will yield to defeat. Negative thoughts are synonymous to depression. Defeating them becomes a constant battle! But one we must win!

Let's look at some scriptural comparisons.

Negative says, "You can't do that. You'll never amount to anything." Phil 4:13 says, "I can do all things through Christ which strengtheneth me."

Negative says, "You are too needy, you can't help yourself." Psalm 40:17 says, "I am poor and needy, yet the Lord thinketh on me."

Negative says, "You are too bad, a waste of time, too messed up." Romans 7:18 says, "For I know that in me (that is in my flesh,) dwelleth no good thing," and then verse 24, 25 reads, "Who shall deliver me from the body of this death. I thank God through Jesus Christ our Lord."

For every negative you can hear, God has a scripture, a promise, or an encouragement, you just have to get in there and dig them out. We will do a lesson on digging for promises! But don't wait. If you are hearing negatives, capture them, write them down. And take them through those three questions—Where did you come from? Are you true? And, where will you take me if I believe you?

And then, find out what God says! Ultimately, you will come back to Proverbs 3:5,6, "Trust in the Lord with all your heart and LEAN NOT TO YOUR OWN UNDERSTANDING." You aren't smart enough to figure everything out – but He is – so simply trust Him for what you don't understand.

Deuteronomy 29:29 is a great verse that taught me that - "The secret things belong unto the Lord our God; but those things which are revealed belong unto us and to our children for ever, that we may do all the words of this law." Some things are secret! But God has revealed plenty enough for us to understand and obey. Trust and obey – right!?

Jeremiah 29:11 tells us God ALWAYS thinks good of and for me. I can positively rest my soul there!

When negatives start – push in that clutch – sing! Praise! Confront it! If you need to, write down the negative thought and deal with it this way –

My mind is saying –
But God's Word says –
So, I will –

Do a study on all the times "I will" is used in Psalms. You will find David had to "I WILL" himself into places! We have to do that sometimes, too! – just by the power of our will, say "NO" to negatives.

And, don't forget your four main tools – Open exposure – if you can't find the positive response from Scripture – ask that friend for help! Call for your mind to be covered by the blood of Christ for protection. Start speaking and singing about God's goodness and love for you.

Narrating is the next thought I studied out. Narrating! There is a problem or situation before you. You are struggling to find a way to voice your opinion, or make your position clear. In your mind you see all the parties involved. Mentally, and sometimes aloud, you rehearse what you would say in that particular situation. Or, you are trying to end a conflict and you practice what you would say. Or you narrate what you wish you had said – but it is too late to go back now.

Let's see what Scripture says. Matthew 12:34-37 reads," O generation of vipers, how can ye, being evil, speak good things? For out of the abundance of the heart the mouth speaketh. A good man out of the good treasure of the heart bringeth forth good things; and an evil man out of the evil treasure bringeth for evil things. But I say unto you, that every idle word that men shall speak, they shall give account thereof in the day of judgment. For by thy words thou shalt be justified, and by thy words thou shalt be condemned."

Did you catch that? Words come from what is in our hearts. We narrate because our heart is boiling! If our heart is good, then good words will be what we hear and speak. If our heart is troublesome, we will hear negative, unhealthy words. But the scariest truth for me, and the one that helped me stop this practice was the last warning

—I must give account before God for every word – my words either justify me or condemn me!

God gets even more emphatic in Proverbs 16:27 when He says," An ungodly man diggeth up evil; and in his lips there is as a burning fire." Digging up evil? That is what we are doing when we continue to narrate – to create words we would say to harm, or to get back at, or even to try to justify our behaviour.

Proverbs 16:6 gives us the remedy. "By mercy and truth iniquity is purged; and by the fear of the Lord men depart from evil." We need to stop and listen to what words are bubbling in our hearts. This is a bad habit that must be broken. And the only tool against it is Prayer! We must confess our self-righteousness, (and that's what narrating is) to God and appeal for forgiveness.

Whatever situation we are trying to address is already known by God and we must believe He is able to take care of it! As we pray, we need to ask God for a right heart attitude. Psalm 51:10, "Create in me a clean heart, O God, and renew a right spirit within me."

We need to agree with God that He is all-wise and we are not. Isaiah 55:8, "For my thoughts are not your thoughts, neither are your ways my ways, saith the Lord."

As we pray, ask the Lord to protect your heart and mind by the blood of Christ – and for Him to remind you to take these situations to Him first. Psalm 119:35, "Make me...make me, to go in the path of thy commandments."

Friend, we could expand on these all so much more, and I challenge you to do some study for yourself. Our thoughts are erratic when we are depressed. They wander in all directions, but if we continue to apply Scripture, and avail ourselves of the tools God has given, He will lead us through the fog into clarity.

Facing Disappointment

Today, I want to share with you what my depression revealed about my heart and what was a turning point for me.

Let me just put it in one word – disappointment. That was the first thing the Lord showed me as I came to rock bottom. The story is kind of funny. And sad.

I had been seriously depressed for about three years. We had arrived on the mission field with hopes high and the first couple of years had gone great. Then, I started feeling frustrated and that's when I began journaling. I wrote and wrote about my feelings and the hurts and disillusionment about being a missionary. But Instead of finding someone to talk to, I kept it bottled up. I put on that brave face and functioned. Meanwhile, inside my four walls, I was a wreck. I cried nearly all day, lost my temper too easily, forgot important things, and felt like a complete failure.

We went on our first furlough, and I prayed for the Lord to find me some help. We travelled and reported to our supporting churches and I kept holding it all in. When we returned to the field, it still hadn't gone away. I kept looking for the key, kept praying and hoping and crying and falling apart.

Then, one day, my friend had all the kids and Tom and I were home alone. He asked me again, as he had many times, "What's wrong." Well, that day it all came tumbling out.

He was sitting in a chair in the corner of the kitchen and I just lost it. I started flogging him – in a controlled way, I didn't want to hurt him, but that's just how I reacted. Totally irrational!

Then the tears started and I was able to open up. I was disappointed and disillusioned. I wasn't able to make missionary life be what I thought it should be. He wasn't doing what I thought he should do. I wasn't doing what I thought I would be doing. Nothing was coming out as I thought it should. And there was the key – I. I thought. I had my plan!

Without realising it, I was trying to design and control, but I wasn't doing a very good job. I was judging Tom according to my ideas, my requirements, my expectations, like I had to make him be a missionary or he should do the things I thought he should do.

It left me disappointed, disillusioned, and very wrong.

I thought that day, that now my depression would go away. I thought that one good cry would fix everything. But again, I thought! It didn't go away immediately. I had built a web of wrong thinking and wrong motives, and now I had to get with the Lord to unpick them, to rebuild my walls!

So, today, I want to talk with you about disappointment. Disappointment is a sadness or a displeasure caused by hopes or expectations that go unfulfilled. It leaves you feeling sad, regretful, despondent, sometimes angry, and heavy-hearted.

Jesus felt disappointment. Do you remember the time He sat on the hillside looking out over Jerusalem? His words were, "O Jerusalem, Jerusalem, thou that killest the prophets, and stonest them which are sent unto thee, how often would I have gathered thy children together, even as a hen gathereth her chickens under her wings, and ye would not" (Matthew 23:37).

He was disappointed with the disciples. Several times Jesus says, "O, ye of little faith." It a really interesting read to look at Jesus' words to the disciples. These guys let Him down often. I'm sure they tested His patience. In Luke 22:32 Jesus tells Peter that He is praying for him – that his faith fails not! It makes me believe Jesus was concerned and disappointed by the lack of the disciples' faith. In John 17 we see Jesus praying for them. He so wanted to see them grow in faith. And, He prays for us. He is our interceder even now! Even when we let Him down, and when we disappoint Him.

So, if Jesus can feel disappointment, we can too! But we don't have to stay there! Let me share with you some quotes and thoughts that I recorded. There is a very interesting book by Zack Eswine entitled Spurgeon's Sorrows. Spurgeon was a man who battled depression most all of his adult life. His sermons are full of advice and the author has pulled together many of Spurgeon's thoughts on the subject.

Spurgeon wrote, "We rightly wonder why God allows depression and other sufferings. (And, we do wonder, don't we?) But let us also wonder why He (Jesus) chooses to suffer it with us and for us." - tempted in all points like as we are! Jesus knows how we feel. And He suffers with us and suffered for us!

Then, the author writes, "No matter how deep you fall, grace goes deeper still. Grace goes deeper no matter what the cause – Jesus is able to sympathize and recover us no matter what we face."

No matter what! 2 Timothy 4:17 says, "Notwithstanding the Lord stood with me, and strengthened me." If my depression is caused by fear, or anger, or disappointment, or whatever, Jesus can meet me and recover me from where I am because He is with me. He is for me!

The main lie of the enemy to those who suffer depression is, "You are alone."
But the excelling truth of our Saviour is, "You are never alone." He is always with you!

God did not promise to give us our desires for health, wealth, and happiness, immunity from trial, or pain in this life. But, He did promise to be <u>with us</u>. Immanuel is His name– God with us!

He is with us – ever present – never to leave or forsake.
He weeps with us.
He celebrates with us.
He helps us.
He strengthens us.
He never lets us go.
He outlasts every evil and terrible thing <u>with us</u> – He carries us through.
He never disappoints us

Jack Eswine says, "These kinds of "with us, for us, understands us, nothing can separate us promises are like berries ripe and ready for our tasting." And they do taste better than disappointment! Right?
The promises of God are yes and amen (2 Cor 1:20). God will have the final word. He is the rescuer who, regardless of our condition to adequately hold on, looks us in the eyes and says, "I will never leave you or forsake you. I am with you. Trust me. Give it to me!"

So, when we face disappointment and disillusionment, let's stop and think about what we are trying to do. Are we trying to make life work the way we want? Are we growing more and more despondent because everything we are trying is failing? Are we feeling alone, or like we are the only one trying?

If so, our depression may be coming from our misplaced ideas and goals. God is with us – we can stop trying to impress Him with our grand ideas! He will not disappoint! He can do exceeding abundantly more than we could ever think or ask. We just have to let Him do the planning and the thinking!

Facing Sorrow

Last visit we looked at disappointment as a possible cause of depression. Today, we are going to talk about sorrow.

The dictionary even defines sorrow as a feeling of deep distress caused by loss, disappointment, or other misfortune. To sorrow is to be sad, miserable, despondent, despairing, to ache, agonize, anguish, suffer. Sounds a lot like depression, doesn't it!

I know sorrow was a part of my depression. Not only had disappointment brought it on, but I had moved countries, said goodbye to my family, and I was trying to assimilate to my new normal. It was like a grieving process. It was a grieving process.

Some people teach grief has seven stages – shock, denial, guilt, anger (bargaining), depression (loneliness and reflection), reconstruction (working it through), acceptance. I found these applied to my depression as well. I faced culture shock. I denied that I had a problem. I felt guilty that I wasn't coping. I was angry about it too, I was depressed, lonely and reflective, but once I opened up – I began to reconstruct my life and accept where I was. I began to thrive again! And you can, too!

You might be somewhere in the spectrum. You don't have to be a missionary to face these types of challenges. We can become sorrowful at the loss of a job, the loss of a loved one, a divorce, a miscarriage. Many things in life cause sorrow. It is normal. But we can't allow ourselves to get stuck there!

In the book I mentioned last time, <u>Spurgeon's Sorrows</u> by Jack Eswine, he takes time to talk about sorrow and the great lessons we can learn. I know there are things I learned during my bout with depression that I could have never learnt as well otherwise. Sometimes we have to get to a point where everything else is blocked out so we can walk through the valley with the Lord and He can be with us and for us and be that light behind the cloud.

Let's look at some of the things we can learn through a time of sorrow.

First, sorrow teaches us a better perspective of what maturity in Jesus looks like. Before my depression, I had this pat idea of what a Christian should look like, how they should sound, where they should go, what they should do—all sorts of laws by which I judged myself and others.

This extreme legalism was part of the guilt trip the enemy used on me. He convinced me that if others knew I was struggling, they wouldn't like me, or believe in me, or trust me. Since I was failing so miserably, I needed to keep myself hidden away, so no one could see.
I wasn't doing anything different or wrong, but my thinking had complete control. It was during this time that the Lord taught me how much He loved me.

He loves me, even if I don't get things right. Even if I fail to read my Bible or pray. Even if I lose my temper or think crazy thoughts – His love for me never changes. He isn't waiting to slap my hand, but take it and lead me to greener pastures because He loves me. And He loves you, too. Maturity in Jesus rests confidently in God's love – no matter what – notwithstanding!

Sorrow also deepens our intimacy with God. He is the only one who can touch our hurting hearts. He feels with us. He puts our tears in a bottle! He binds up our wounds. He comforts our soul. He knows us inside and out – and loves us to the end. He is the lover of our soul!

That intimacy is what brought me to Job 13:15, "Though he slay me, yet will I trust him." I remember the day I lay on my bed crying and praying. I repeated this verse and told the Lord, "If I have to be depressed for the remainder of my time on this earth, I will stay true and trust you." That type of intimacy does not take place without being driven into the wilderness.

Sorrow shed our pretences. It brings us to self-examination. As you work through depression/sorrow, you need to do some self-examination. Judge yourself – according to His word. Spurgeon wrote, "When your house has been made to shake, it causes you to see whether it is founded upon a rock."

You won't come through depression the same person – you can't! God is doing a work on your life and yielding is necessary. If you keep covering it up, denying it, or putting on that brave face, you aren't progressing. So, shed those pretences.

Like we have talked about – use James 5:16 – go find someone to talk to – be honest with them – be honest with the Lord – be honest with yourself! Don't be afraid! You won't bottom out! God is still there – He already knows what you are pretending to be and He's waiting for you to invite Him to help.

Sorrow exposes and roots out pride. I know this was one of the hardest lessons I had to learn through my depression. I thought I had everything worked out, but depression tore my confidence to shreds.

Spurgeon wrote – "We sometimes rise too high, in our own estimation, that unless the Lord took away some of our joy, we should be utterly destroyed by pride." God took me through His word to look at pride as I healed. I was amazed at the hold it had on my life.

Pride is when you look at someone else and think you are better looking, better dressed, smarter, or any superior thought. You might never say it, never act like it, but just the fact that you thought it is proof of your pride.
Pride is when you wait for others to mention your name in a conversation, or from the pulpit, or in the classroom.
Pride is when you push your agenda on others, when you feel your way is always best, or when you manipulate others to get your way.
Pride is very subtle. We ALL deal with it. And, it is one of the things God says, He hates.

How does sorrow expose and root out pride? Because it leaves us little to nothing to be proud about. What's to be proud about crying in bed all day, or trying to hide, or feeling angry and frustrated? There's nothing to be proud of in those things.

Sorrow also teaches us empathy – we start to understand how others feel by what we have experienced. Once we come through sorrow or depression, we are better equipped to help others. We gain a second-sense into the words people say, the look on their faces, and the habits of their lives. God uses sorrow for our benefit, and the benefit of others.

2 Corinthians 1:3, 4 "Blessed be God...the God of all comfort; who comforteth us in all our tribulation, that we may be able to comfort them which are in any trouble, by the comfort wherewith we ourselves are comforted of God." That's exactly why we are having this discussion isn't it? To help each other!

As we are talking about depression and especially about building walls, it is important that we understand about our thought life and learn thought control. We need to find the cause of our depression, be it disappointment, sorrow, anger, hurts, loss, or whatever, and continue using God's Word to combat our malady.

Sorrows are caused by ugly things. But Jesus brings them to be used for our benefit.
He is the Man of Sorrows. He is their master. No matter what fiendish thought or unexplainable cause gave them birth, He invites us to receive healing from Him.

Dear friend, bring your sorrow, your depression, your disappointment or disillusionment to Him! He is the God of all comfort!

The Enemy Within

Today I want to visit with you about what I believe to be
the hardest truth about depression, and thee thing none
of us want to admit, that most depression is based in self.
It is over-thought of self.

Now, bear with me. I want to explain this as clearly and as
kindly as I can.
And I need you to remember that I have been there, so
let's talk honestly for a while.

When we are depressed, we focus on our feelings, right?
But here's the truth – when we face an emergency, those
feelings go away until the emergency was over. That alone
shows us that our feelings can change. And, that we are
being deceived by them.

Instead of getting on our knees, we justify our feelings,
dwell on them, and entertain them because for some
strange reason we think they make us feel better – really?

We are so sad that we get used to feeling sad.
We are so angry that we feel we must be angry.
We are so anxious that we think we must be anxious or
something is wrong.

We look around for things to keep our feelings going
instead of laying them at the foot of the cross and
denouncing them.

From there, Habits develop – we start lying, being late for
work, not doing the housework, over spending, over
working, or withdrawing. These habits become ingrained

and we think we can never break the cycle. There's another of those never and always lies!

We start accepting lies. I've made too big of a mess, I'm no good, I'm useless. We start building our lives around these lies instead of taking them through the three questions, claiming the blood of Christ, or seeking a friend who will pray. We want to change our feelings and actions, but we are not addressing the force that is sucking out our strength. And did you notice the first word in each of those statements? I - I am no good, I am never going to get better, I am alone I, I, I....?

There is an amazing little book called We Neurotics by Bernard Basset. It is a funny story of one man's path through depression. You will be surprized by some of what he says, but he nails depression on the head saying, "Broadly speaking, the more you think, the more you think about yourself."

That is why we need thought control. Self needs to be put in its place.

"But, Gail, you say, I'm not thinking of myself? I have a real problem."

Okay, ask yourself then, what is your first thought in the morning? What are your thoughts as you prepare for the day, as you travel to work, as you go through your day?

"Most of us will have to admit that our preferences, our annoyances, our self-image, and fears make up the majority of our thought time." Bernard Basset continues, "I would say that all scruples, fear, religious mania, melancholy, hatred, and impurity are based on the inability to control our thoughts. This is the supreme form of self-centeredness. "

Why are we so self-centered? Because we are sinners, right? Because we want control? Yes. Because we want recognition, acceptance, appreciation, etc.? Yes.

My will for power is very great. My ambition causes me to over work and put undue pressure on myself. If I feel I am failing to get what I want or reach my goal or be who I think I should be, I regress into excuses. I don't want to admit my own failure – that is pride.

I want to save face, so I use comments like, I would have succeeded but....I had bad health, a cruel father, prejudice against me, or was too poor, when all we really need to do is humble ourselves before God, confess our pride as sin, and allow child-like faith and obedience to carry us through.

These excuses usually come in the form of words starting with the prefix dis – disappointment, disillusionment, disagreeable, dissatisfaction – dis indicates duplicity and duplicity means conflict, indecision, and unhappiness. Because, we cannot serve two masters.

It is the duplicity of our hearts and the painful conflict between God and self that we are experiencing in depression.

Sadly, we bring this same struggle into our prayer life. We pray about our troubles.... did you catch that? our troubles

– even our prayer time becomes self-centred. It becomes a pity party – it's my party and I'll cry if I want to.

Hosea 7:14 talks about the silliness of not crying to the Lord with our heart, but just howling upon our beds. We are guilty of nursing it and rehearsing it instead of cursing it and reversing it. So, what are we to do with our self-centeredness?

Mainly, we need to learn thought control. We have talked about that. Our thought life is where our will and pride have free reign. We spend too much time thinking and mooning about ourselves – what will make me happy, what will make me look good, how can I get to the top of the pile, why doesn't anyone love me, why do I always fail, why can't I be like everyone else, why don't people accept me...me, me, me, me, I, I, I.

When I was able to accept the truth about my thought life, it made a real change for me. I started hearing what I was thinking, and I noticed how often my thoughts were self-centred. That is when I began working through those N's of the Night that we talked about.

If I wanted to get control of my thoughts, I couldn't just **not** think about myself, I had to replace my thoughts – renew my mind as the Lord tells us in Romans 12. And that meant replacing the negative with positive. And not just those little platitudes about how much God loves me, accepts me, values me...because that is still self-focus...but replacing them with truth about God. Replacing them with praise of Him, thanksgiving. When I did that, I started gaining and my walls started going up!

Then, start thinking of others – as Jesus did – do a good deed, practice the golden rule, be kind and thoughtful.

I took some simple scriptures and began putting them into practice each day. Like – "Love thinketh no evil." When I was tempted with an evil or unkind thought, I resisted it and chose to change it to a kind thought. I pushed in that clutch and changed gears!

I began choosing to do good, to do the most loving thing I could think of for those around me. Oh, sometimes self would grow weary, think it didn't really matter, or get angry because my kindness wasn't being recognized, but there again – that was my will resisting my efforts to renew my mind. It takes concentrated effort to grow new thought paths, but it is possible!

I even went as far as asking forgiveness from those I had hurt.

I remember one day I said something that I felt was off handed or unkind to one of the mothers in our neighbourhood. It was still very depressed at this time and just starting to come to the light, but I believed my words could have been hurtful, and I felt the Lord wanted me to apologize. I really didn't know her well, but I knew where she lived.

So, with a huge spiritual battle going on in my head and heart, I marched myself down there and asked her to forgive me for my words. She looked at me like I had lost my mind (I think I was near that point). But she assured me of her forgiveness and asked me in.

I don't remember anything that was said that day, but I do remember walking home knowing I had just turned a corner. No longer could my thoughts accuse and control me. I had obeyed by faith and God had met me there. Because of me? No, because I put her feelings above mine, swallowed my pride, and obeyed God.

Maybe you need to make some things right with people who have been hurt by your words or actions. Are you going to continue thinking how bad you have it, or reach out and think of the feelings of others? It's hard stuff, but it was definitely a turning point for me.

It isn't that you will never think of yourself, but there must be balance. Love thy neighbour as thyself. Remember, other people live here, too!

Depression is an over focus on self to the disregard of others – a pity party of one. No one else allowed and we put up barriers to keep an imagined safety net. But it isn't a safety net, it is a booby trap.

So, what are we to do?

1. Rebuild those walls –
    Romans 12:2 – be transformed by the renewing of your mind
    2 Corinthians 10:5 - bringing every thought captive to – obedience!
    Start building strong Scriptural walls!
2. And Relax - let your mind rest. Stop the droning. Listen to good Christian music and be still. Think on God – think on beauty… pray with praise and thanksgiving. Self wants all the attention –self

wants the throne! but self is not worthy! Only He is worthy! God needs to be on the throne of your heart and mind! Think on Him!

3. Take one step at a time...brick by brick. That's how you build a wall!! Conquer each thought!

Your walls will go up and your will begin to heal as you conquer the enemy within.

Four Depressed Men

Let's visit one more time on some of the causes of depression. We have mentioned disappointment, sorrow, and the enemy within, but today, I want us to look at four men in the Bible who experienced depression.

No one would be surprised if I say that comments or thoughts like, "I've had it. I've failed and will never succeed. I want to die" are part of the internal voice.

All of the men we will look at today are Bible heroes. For three of them, their internal voices said the same thing. Matter of fact, they actually said those words out loud! "I want to die." And brave enough to say this to God! But the fourth one had a different response.

The man who was used of God to bring Egypt to her knees, wrote the first five books of the Old Testament and knew God face to face said, "I want to die." His name was **Moses.**

The man who survived three days and three nights in the belly of a whale, preached to the world's most wicked nation and saw a great revival said, "I want to die." His name was **Jonah.**

The man who could pray down drought and rain, raise the dead, feed the living, rebuke the king, and call fire from heaven said, "I want to die." His name was **Elijah.**

I'm thankful our Lord wasn't too ashamed of His servants to hide the truth from us. I'm so glad their record is there so we can draw hope for ourselves. It's a hard thing to admit you are suffering with depression. You hear things like, "It is a sin to be depressed. Spiritual people never experience depression. Mental illness is always a sign of demon possession. Good Christians never need counselling." All of these are false!

There is no need for us to suffer in silence when the Wonderful Counsellor has spoken openly about our situation! Again – get brave – practice James 5:16...it's a biblical thing to do! Find someone to pray with.

God understands depression. He knows it causes mood swings, feelings of inadequacy, and a whole group of curious feelings of failure, even when we are seeing spiritual success. Even when we can't see why in the world we should feel this way. I think that's why it is so confusing.

Causes and symptoms will vary, but there are some general characteristics that apply to all of us.

1. Anyone can get depressed – even Christians.
2. Depression is not terminal – it is not a deadly disease of itself.
3. It is always temporary – It may take time, but you will get better.
4. Depression often requires help. So, don't be too proud to ask for it!
5. Using medication is not a lack of faith!
6. Depression is common – right! All temptations are common...but God is faithful!
7. Depression can be dangerous. If left unaddressed, it can lead to destructive life patterns.

There are different types of depression –
Organic – those caused by things happening in and to our bodies. You need to have a check with the doctor. Make sure things are right with your body clock!
Neurotic – those caused by emotional shock – things that throw us into a tailspin.
And Reactive – those triggered by a circumstance or event causing a sense of loss or failure or frustration.

Now, let's go back to those first three men – for all of them, their depressions were reactive – triggered by what was happening.

Moses had an impossible workload, the constant griping of the Israelites over the water and food supplies, the forced march through the dessert, along with the constant threat of an enemy ambush. It finally got to him.

What were his symptoms? He was fatigued, discouraged and wanted to give up. He was tired of the workload – burn out we could call it! In Numbers 11:14, 15 he says to God, "I am not able to bear all this people alone, because it is too heavy for me. And if thou deal thus with me, kill me, I pray thee."

What was God's counsel? First – learn to delegate! Second – God took care of feeding the people – He sent the quail.

If you feel like Moses, you must learn to say no to extra responsibilities, enlist the help of others, withdraw from high-pressured demands. Chop that to-do list down to bite-size portions and learn to lean more heavily on the resources available with God. He will carry you through.

He will give you the strength to accomplish the appointment He has given.

You might be burning out because you are unwilling to delegate, or think you must carry the whole load. Matthew 11:28-30 says, "Come unto me, all ye that labor and are heavy laden, and I will give you rest. Take my yoke upon you and learn of me, for I am meek and lowly in heart and ye shall find rest unto your souls. for my **yoke is easy and my burden is light.**"
Come back to the Lord when you feel overworked and let Him give you rest.

Elijah was exhausted physically, spiritually, and emotionally. He had just confronted the prophets of Baal, called fire down from heaven and run seventeen miles to escape the wrath of Queen Jezebel. He felt deserted by his friends and all alone.

What did he say to God? From underneath the juniper tree he cried out, "It is enough; now, O Lord, take away my life; for I am not better than my fathers." 1 Kings 19:4

What did God do? He put Elijah to sleep, fed him, encouraged him, reminded him that he was not alone, and then changed his job description.

If you feel like Elijah, let God change things around for you, learn to rest in the God of all comfort, and then, get back to work----even if it means taking a different position or a step down from the current pressure.

Psalm 34:19 – "Many are the afflictions of the righteous, but the Lord delivereth them out of them all." Let the Lord deliver you!

And our third man is Jonah. He was angry, bewildered and embarrassed. He had constructed his own system of beliefs that now left him confused.

I think this is where I was! My thinking was mixed up and my belief system had been jarred. Things weren't as I thought they should be! Well, it was a similar thing for Jonah –

He believed disobedience deserved death— throw me overboard – I'd rather die than obey God, yet he disobeyed and survived.
He believed whale attacks were fatal—yet he was swallowed alive and lived.
He believed wicked nations would be destroyed—yet Nineveh all was spared.
He believed God could not love the Ninevites—yet God did love them and forgive them.
It left him angry, because his whole belief system had been upset. God was not acting as Jonah thought God should act.

What did he say to God? "I do well to be angry, even unto death. It is better for me to die than to live." Jonah 4:8, 9

What did God do? Again, God was merciful to His despairing prophet. God offered him comfort in the form of the gourd bush (a shade from the beating sun), but Jonah was so angry he did not see it from the hand of God. He refused God's counsel, so he received a rebuke. God

reminded him that the eternal souls of the Ninevites were of greater value than the temporary bush that had shaded him. Jonah didn't want to change his thinking!
Sometimes in depression we are the same. We think our idea is right and God is wrong.

If you feel like Jonah, you need to realign your beliefs to God word, look and see God's goodness around you, learn gratitude and thankfulness, and begin loving others as you love yourself---start seeing people as God sees them!

So, reactive depression is caused by circumstances or events that provoke pressure and pain that we feel we don't deserve. We blame God, we pity ourselves, and we withdraw into a dark stupor or begin to pout!

Now, let's look at our fourth man. King David. He was depressed, but for a different reason. David's depression was a reactive spiritual depression. The Bible calls it despair, we call it guilt. Unresolved guilt results in depression. David was overwhelmed by the guilt of his sins of adultery and murder. He refused to eat and lost his energy and vitality.

But what David said to God is very different than the other three men's responses. David admitted his sin when confronted. 2 Samuel 12:13, "I have sinned against the Lord."

What did God do? He forgave David.

So, let's bring our visit down to a few simpler phrases.

If you are overworked like Moses, learn to delegate and lean on the Lord.

If you are embattled like Elijah, get some rest and look at changing your position or job.

If you are disappointed and angry like Jonah, ask God to correct your attitude and beliefs.

If you are guilty of sin like David, seek God's forgiveness through confession and repentance and let Him restore you.

I want to share with you two more verses that became tools to my heart. The first one is Psalm 118:17, 18 "I shall not die, but live, and declare the works of the Lord. The Lord hath chastened me sore: but he hath not given me over unto death."

When I was depressed, I took that phrase as my mantra as I healed – "I shall not die, but live and declare the works of the Lord." It's what I call futurizing – looking beyond the circumstances of today to the hope of what will be tomorrow. I am here before you today as proof of this promise.

And the other verse is Psalm 42:5 – "Why art thou cast down, O my soul? And why art thou disquieted in me? – Find the cause! It might be disappointment, sorrow, anger, overwork, being embattled, worry, wrong thinking, or an outright sin, but find the cause, and there could be more than one.

Then, go forward with hope!

"Hope thou in God: for I shall yet praise him for the help of his countenance." The Wonderful Counsellor will meet you! He will help you! Depression is temporary. It may take time, but you will get better!

Psalm 34:22 – "The Lord redeemeth the soul of his servants and none of them that trust in Him shall be desolate." You will live and not die! Hope thou in God!

Can Christians Be Depressed

It might seem like an odd question, but depressed Christians, often feel immense guilt. They believe they should not feel like this. But ask yourself --Can a Christian feel pain? Can a Christian sin? Can a Christian be un-Christian-like? Of course!

Just because we have placed our faith in Christ, that does not remove us from the feelings and interruptions of life in this old sinful world. We are still human. Bad and sad things still happen. So, yes, a Christian can be depressed.

Depression, with its many causes and symptoms, is not sin in and of itself. It is a reaction, or a result, as we mentioned last time. It is reactive (to circumstance), neurotic (shock) or organic (physical cause), but it always has a source.

I think the really hard thing about depression is finding the cause, then, working your way back to health. This is where we get stuck! We have woven such a web of wrong thinking that we feel like we are taking one step forward and two steps back! We will never be right again.

And, sometimes, we can get so deep into depression that we cry out for the Lord to take us, even like the Bible men we talked about last visit. They were definitely Christian – and yet they wanted relief from depression!

Let me give you a quote and we will talk about this a bit more. Jack Eswine says, "Those in deep depression exalt themselves to a place of knowledge and importance. They assume an all-knowing posture; declaring all possible and future good have died to them. Their misery poisons them with tragic arrogance. Pain deludes their reason. From a god-like vantage point, they tragically and misguidedly declare they will never see good again. All-or-nothing posture infiltrates their convictions drowning them in selfishness. In this, they deny the present and future power of Christ."

There a lot in that quote, but what he is saying is when depression has complete control, we don't see any way out. Because we can't figure it out ourselves, we deny Christ's power to help us. That is complete selfishness! It's back to "I" – I must solve my problem. I can't find my way out.

When we are depressed, we become convinced that
1. Circumstances are too hard and life will always be bad.
2. People are terrible.
3. I can't live with my failure or without some particular person.
4. I'm embarrassed at my weakness. I can never show my face again.
5. I'm mistreated, misunderstood, unwanted, etc. No one will ever love me – a big pity party!
6. I'm too old and set in my ways – nothing new could happen for me.
7. I didn't get what I wanted...if I can't have it, then there is no point – my way or no way.
8. I'm guilty. I've done terrible things. I will never recover from the wrong I've done.

Do you see all the negative thoughts? All the never and always comments?

That is the main thing in depression – negative thoughts! Thoughts that convince us of the enemy's lies. And if we believe them, we will continue on the downward spiral.

Those statements need to be altered! And we can do that by using the three questions – Where did you come from? Are you true? Where will you take me if I believe you?

I've even got a little book out using those three questions to teach children to think through their thoughts. It's called There's a Hole in My Sock. Its available online. The main character, Mikey, uses those three questions to sort a negative nagging thought that won't stop playing in his head. It's a simple teaching, but very effective for children, and adults.

Let's just take one or two of those eight statements and go through them.

1. Circumstances are too hard and life will always be bad.
    a. Where did you come from?
        1) You might have come because I am facing hard times.
        2) You might have come because I am disappointed or tired.
        3) You might have come because I've been fighting a long hard battle.
    b. Are you true?
        1) Yes, circumstances can be genuinely hard.

2) And, No – life will not always be bad – there are happy spots! Things will get better. I can look for the sunny side!

3) And, No – too hard? God has promised not to give me more than He is able to help me carry. He is always there for me. Isaiah 45:2,3 reads, "I will go before thee, and make the crooked places straight: I will break in pieces the gates of brass, and cut in sunder the bars of iron: And I will give thee the (GET THIS) <u>treasures of darkness</u>, and <u>hidden riches of secret places."</u> Treasure and riches where? In darkness and secret places – God has something for you in your circumstances.

The verse continues ---"that thou mayest know that I, the Lord, which call thee by thy name, am the God of Israel." He is going to meet you there! To reveal more of Himself to you! That alone is a great treasure!

c. Where will you take me if I believe you?

1) Obviously, you will keep discouraging me.

2) You will cause me to give up—to stop looking for help.

3) I could lose my job, or my marriage, or my family.

So, I need to resist and place my focus on Christ's promise. Jeremiah 29:11, "For I know the thoughts that I think toward you, saith the Lord, thoughts of peace, and not of evil, to give you an expected end."

He will carry you through and give treasures of darkness and hidden riches of secret places – right where you are! Just trust Him!

2. I'm guilty, I've done terrible things. I can never recover from the wrong I have done.
    a. Where did you come from?
        1) I've done something wrong – lied, stole, whatever it might be.
        2) The enemy is reminding me of my failure.
        3) God might be convicting me—drawing me to confession and repentance. I need to yield! To deal with my guilt and stop denying it. Proverbs 28:13 – "He that covereth his sins shall not prosper; but whoso confesseth and forsaketh them shall have mercy."
    b. Are you true?
        1) Yes, I may have done something wrong. I might be guilty of something.
        2) No, I can recover. God can forgive and heal my life.
        3) No, I can make things right – pay my debt, ask forgiveness, take responsibility and learn to be accountable.
    c. Where will you take me if I believe you?
        1) I will want to hide for fear of being found out.
        2) I might grow angry at the restrictions I feel from my unresolved guilt.
        3) I might give up and just go deeper into crime because I lose hope.

Again, resist using God's truth – 1 John 1:9, "If we confess our sins, He is faithful and just to forgive us our sins and to cleanse us from ALL unrighteousness." We don't have to allow sin to separate us from God's favor or drive us to depression.

You can take any lie of the enemy through those three questions and start to help yourself. You can also take them to that trusted friend and ask them to help you think the questions through. Remember to watch out for those negative thoughts and especially those ones that include the words always and never – they are Never Always true!

God has mercy for every trial. So, can a Christian be depressed? Yes, they can.

But, for the Christian there is a hope that abounds! There is a Saviour who was tempted in all points like as we are, yet without sin.

You might feel depressed, be crying in your bed and feel like a waste of time, but God sees you as His child. He will meet you by the river, under the Juniper tree, on the hillside above Nineveh, or even in the cave where you have gone to hide. He is the Wonderful Counselor and He will not leave His children to flounder in the wilderness forever!

Like He said to Hagar, "What aileth thee, Hagar? Fear not; for God hath heard." Or like he asked Elijah, "What doest thou here?" God calls His children to answer.

He does not leave them desolate! "Many are the afflictions of the righteous: but the Lord delivereth him out of them all" Psalm 34:19. "The Lord redeemeth the soul of his servants, and none of them that trust in Him shall be desolate." Vs 22.

Recovery can take time, but you can get better! You will stand again! God has more planned for you.
1 Corinthians 2:9, "Eye hath not seen, nor ear heard, neither have entered into the heart of man, the things which God hath prepared for them that love him."

I am testimony to that fact! And, many others will attest to the same! Keep walking dear friend. God isn't finished with you yet!

Futurizing

Remember those four men who suffered depression—
Moses because of overwork. Elijah because of battles,
Jonah because of a faulty belief system, anger, and
disobedience, and David because of sin?

But there is another man whose journey through
depression is well documented. He was a man God
declared virtuous and upright. A man above men, but he
found himself at a total loss to discover why such hard
times had come. And, he also wished to die –that man's
name was Job.

Job 6:8-9 "Oh, that I might have my request; and that God
would grant me the thing that I long for: Even that it would
please God to destroy me; that he would let loose his hand
and cut me off."

Job knew, even though he felt so low and deserted, that
God's hand held him!

There are many other beautiful gems of faith and hope
throughout the book of Job.

Job 13:15 – "Though he slay me, yet will I trust him."
Job 1:21 – "The Lord giveth and the Lord taketh away,
blessed be the name of the Lord."
Job 19:25 – "I know that my Redeemer lives."
Job 19:26 – "I shall see God."

God held Job together with these truths. And in all the
surmising of his friends, in all this sadness and
wonderment, Job sinned not.

In the end, we can see two blessed things that should encourage us when we face situations where we cannot see the why or how.

First, God was not going to leave Job where he was. God was on His way. He didn't feel sorry for Job, and just pat him on the head, but God showed His wonderful power and wisdom. He revealed His prerogative in directing Job's life and brought Job to see the hand of God – the hand under which Job needed to submit – to humble himself – to agree with God that all Job's words and thoughts were minuscule compared to God—to get Job back into his place.

It's sort of the same thing God tried to show to Jonah, but Jonah did not want to submit.

The other thing I see in Job's story is that his future was secure. God's blessing was reserved for him, even though Job could not see it. At the end of the story, Job is rewarded double for everything he lost.

How many times have we experienced what we felt was total loss, only to be rewarded by the Lord in unimaginable ways? And when that happens, we must fall on our knees in gratitude and recognize the undeserved mercy and blessing of God.

If you are in the middle of depression or strenuous circumstance, remember that God knows where you are. He's coming, and He will arrive at just the right moment. Your future is secure, even if you can't see it. Keep going by faith and in humility. You serve a great God whom you can trust – no matter what!

I want us to look at another thing I learned through depression. I call it futurizing. To do this, we need to have scripture fully in our mind.

Let's start with the verse from Job 1:21 – "The Lord giveth and the Lord taketh away."

Look at your current situation. What has the Lord given you? What has He removed?
You start planning for the future with what you have right now. You can't hope to be the CEO of a company if you haven't the education that goes behind it. You can't hope to become a concert pianist without hours of practice. Be realistic.

Job was realistic. He had been given a wonderful family, wealth, and prestige, but all of this had been taken away. He had to start from where he was, a diseased man in the dust.

Sometimes we can feel that low, too. When you read Job's words, you don't read about him wallowing in what he had lost in the matter of earthly goods. In one verse he longs for his lost family, but the remainder of his words look to the why of his situation. It was the loss of the fellowship with God that troubled him most.

Is that what troubles you? The loss of God's fellowship, or is it the loss of convenience, friendships, control, or material things? Or best future depends on an increased fellowship with God. Not the number of things we can reaccumulate. Without that precious fellowship, all these things are of little comfort. They can be taken away again. So, let's establish that things are temporal. God is eternal. Our future is securely in His hands.

David wrote in Psalm 118:17, 18 "I shall not die, but live, and declare the works of the Lord. The Lord hath chastened me sore: but he hath not given me over unto death."

When I was depressed, this verse really hit my heart – "I shall not die, but live and declare the works of the Lord." That is what brought me to futurizing – looking beyond the circumstance of today to the hope of what will be tomorrow.

It is another of those "I will" verses that are so powerful in aiding your will to find overcoming strength in low times. Take time to look at each of the "I will" verses in Psalms and let them build your hope and resolve. My blog, Beside the Well, lists several in the devotion entitled Deliberate Calculations.

"I will" verses are the ones that help us deliberately calculate our actions and choices. I will sing. I will pray. I will praise. I will not fear—beautiful verses that give hope for the future and an attitude that will take you there.

They are matched with the "I wills" of God – I will redeem you, I will hear when you cry, I will give you peace, I will answer, I will be your strength. You'll find many more of these in Psalms as well. You can build your future and your walls on these promises!

Now, let's go to Colossians 3 – "set your affections on things above." If we are going to futurize, make plans, set our hopes on what God could make out of our awful place, we must set our hearts on more than temporal relief. Our focus, our love, and our desires need to be set on higher goals rather than the immediate solution.

I'm not talking about being pious or spiritually high-minded, but being more attached to the things God would want to make of my life than the things I am crying about because I can't or don't have. It is a change of focus that helps us build walls of strength in Christ and avoid building something of our own making – that straw house that the wolf can blow down.

Set your affection is a phrase relating to thought control. To me, it means looking forward with hope and anticipation– looking toward a goal – to fix your eyes and your heart – Psalm 57:7 – "My heart is fixed, O God, my heart is fixed: I will sing and give praise!" I will do it now and I will do it in the future because my affections are set on God!

Before we look at the last scripture for today, let's put these three together.

We need to accept and understand God's prerogative in giving and taking – our times are in His hands – He is God, we are not. We are where we are, and God knows where we are! His hand is holding us no matter what!

God has a plan for us – we will not die, but live - and not to live for ourselves, but to tell others of how great God is –

what He had done for us. The word of our testimony will be used to help others!

To do this, we need the right thought – the right attitude – the right affections – set on God, and determination, the "I will" to get through depression and more toward our goals.

What does futurizing look like?

For me, it meant seeing myself back on my feet – spiritually, physically, and emotionally. To be able to make it through one day without feeling low or battling negative thoughts.
Then, to make it from Sunday to Sunday without a dip in the middle.

My futurizing (which includes goals, hopes, and dreams) began to grow and God allowed me to do things I didn't even believe were possible. Like what I'm doing today! I would never have dreamed I would be doing this! But this is where God has brought me!

For you, it could mean different things. I worked with one lady who struggled with alcohol. By futurizing, she moved toward victory. Her goals were to own her own home again, to learn to drive, and to be able to take care of her family.

To futurize, you set yourself two or three realistic goals. Then, set your affection, your attention, your "I Will" on those. Each little victory helps pull you forward.

It's like watching those walls go up! Setting the capstones and securing the mortar!

Is it that easy? Well, some days it is! And some days it is not. That's when I fall back on this last scripture. Psalm 27:13, 14

"I had fainted, unless I had believed to see the goodness of the Lord in the land of the living. Wait on the Lord: be of good courage, and he shall strengthen thine heart: wait, I say, on the Lord."

I had fainted – I would have given up, if I had not believed to see the goodness of the Lord in the land of the living – the land of the living! Right now – and in the future!

I shall not die, but live! And tell the goodness of the Lord! God will help me make it, even when I feel like fainting. Even when some days, I fail. I can start again the next morning because His mercies are renewed day by day! He will give me the courage and strength I need while I wait for my future.

What does your future look like? Can you see beyond today? Or are your affections set on the dust in which you sit? Look up, dear friend!

God is still there. Your future is secure. Your redeemer lives, and because of Him, you will too! Reach forward to the things ahead of you and press toward that mark!

Blueprints and Diamonds

Let's take a good look at where we are in our discussion about depression.

We started working at building up our walls, remember? Proverbs 16:32 and 25:28. "He that hath no rule over his own spirit is like a city that is broken down and without walls."

We looked at finding the cause and being able to admit we were depressed.

We have talked several times about using the tools of confession and James 5:16. We considered claiming the blood of Christ, the word of your testimony, and self-sacrifice from Revelation 12:11. And we have worked through the three questions. Where did you come from? Are you true? Where will you take me if I believe you?

We looked at the N's of the Night and the precious promises of God. We discussed disappointment, sorrow, and depressed Christians. We talked about the enemy within – our self that wants control and how God counselled His men when they felt so low they wanted to die.

Last visit, we learned about futurizing and that our future is secure in His hands.

Today, we are going to take some of these tools and start to put bricks and mortar to our walls.

Let's start with this scripture – "In the multitude of my thoughts within me, thy comforts delight my soul" (Psalm 94:19).

God knows we are thinkers! We plan, we hope, we desire. These are natural attributes of humanity. But sometimes, our thinking takes over, creating worry.

Sorrow looks back, Worry looks around, but Faith looks forward, right!?

So, if thinking is our nemesis, let's put it to work instead of letting it wander uncontrolled!

You can't build without a plan, so we need to look at what we hope to build.

God's word gives us many clues. As a matter of fact, God is rather specific when He gives building instructions. Have you ever read the blueprint for the tabernacle or Solomon's temple? God doesn't miss a detail. If He is that concerned about a building, imagine how concerned He is about your life – your building – your walls?

One of the first things you will see in your blueprint is the promises of God. You can't ignore them. They give assurance and support to your walls. They are like the mortar that holds truth in place. Like architectural directions, the promises of God reveal the proposed structure.

Spurgeon wrote, "The secret hope of a man is a truer test of his condition before God than the acts of any one day, or even the public devotions of a year. A story larger and truer than our moods or miseries holds us."

And that secret up is the truth of God's word – His promises to us! We have an image – a secret hope – of what life will be like once we are out of depression. (Futurizing, right?) And God knows that image. Even though we may struggle and fail as we build, His promise remains. We are more than the trials, feelings, or choices of a moment might suggest about us.

My life's verse is Philippians 1:6 – "He that began a good work in you will perform it." God is doing a work in me. And Colossians says, "For it is God that worketh in you both to will and to do of his good pleasure." God is making something of my life, according to His blueprint.

This is where you need to start mining for promises that bring your thoughts and desires into line with what God is doing.

Is He calling you to be a better mother?
Is He asking you to learn more about controlling your tongue?
Is He trying to teach you patience, or faith, or wisdom?

There is always a lesson to learn in depression.

Whatever He is teaching you, whatever work He is trying to do for you and in you, you will find promises to cling to. They are the mortar that holds everything together! You need to find them.

Like any miner, some days, you find nothing, but then a jewel drops into your hand, "in due season, a promise presents itself, which seems to have been made for the occasion; it fits as exactly as a well-made key," Spurgeon says. Those promises are yours! They are the ones with which you build.

It's rare to find jewels just lying on the ground waiting to be picked up. The most valuable ones must be mined. The same is true for the promises of God. Sometimes, one will fall from the pulpit or pop up while you are reading scripture, but the ones of most value are revealed by agony of heart and a deeper understanding of the word.

When we take on the promises of God, we take up with Him. But the promise isn't something we have created, they are His promises, and we use them.

We can use them in prayer. As we pray the promises of God, they are driven deeper into our hearts and thoughts.

So how do you pray a promise of God? We mentioned it before.

Dear Lord, I'm tempted to believe _____. But your word says _____. So, I will_____.

This is what I WILL do based on your promise.

Or—Dear Lord, I am so thankful you have promised to _____. Help me now to place my trust fully in the promise of Your word while I wait for you to _____.

He has promised His word will not return void – it will accomplish its goal.

And for you, in depression, the goal is healing and rebuilding your life. So, mine for promises that bring strength, confidence, and assurance.
Write them on your heart and put them on your fridge, memorize and meditate – that's how you build! Jude 20, 21 reads, "But ye, beloved, building up yourselves on your most holy faith, praying in the Holy Ghost, Keep yourselves in the love of God." SET YOUR AFFECTIONS ON GOD!

Another thing about building – it needs order. You can't put on the roof before you have the walls, and you can't put in the glass before you have the window frame. Sometimes depression leaves us with our building material scatters and our tools in the wrong places.

We talked a bit about self-examination, and this is where this comes in. We need to look at what we are doing that inhibits our building project. We have to put off some things and put on some new things.

Ephesians 4:22-24 says, "That ye put off concerning the former conversation the old man, which is corrupt according to the deceitful lusts; And be renewed in the spirit of your mind; And that ye put on the new man, which after God is created in righteousness and true holiness."

Put off – leave behind the stuff that brought you down, and put on the stuff God has prepared. There is a good book called Leaving Yesterday Behind by W.L. Hines that clearly teaches this principle. We can't go into the whole thing here, but this book is a perfect place to start if you need help in this area.

Another thing you can do is look at your life patterns. Let me explain a couple of exercises you can do to discover problem patterns that may be keeping you depressed or feeling low.

Make yourself a little chart. Make one square for each day and divide each day into morning, afternoon, and evening. For one week, carefully list all events, situations or activities (good or bad) that resulted in causing you to feel depressed, or get angry, or have uncontrolled thoughts – whatever thing you are working on.

Then, at the end of the week, look back to see if there are recurring events or times when you are more vulnerable. Those tell you things to watch out for – things to put off and where you need to look for new coping mechanisms.

Another building exercise is to teach yourself how to solve problems. Every building faces challenges! Some are costly! So, a good builder keeps checks along the way!

There are four questions to answer in this exercise.
1. **What happened** – describe the problem.
2. **What I did** – how did you respond?
3. **What I could have done** – what would have been the biblical response – forgive, keep quiet, etc.
4. **What I must do now.** Describe the steps you must take to rectify the matter – ask forgiveness, remove yourself from the situation, swallow your pride, face your fears, and make things right.

This exercise teaches you how to continue building. Every time you obey God's directives, you gain strength, and you will be renewing your mind and making those walls stronger and more secure.

Here's the thing, though, you can't go around giving yourself an out or using an excuse. To build strong walls, you need to give your infraction a biblical term and find a biblical alternative with scripture references to create a record of your build. That way, you will have tools you can implement to beautify and repair your walls for the rest of your life.

If you need help finding your way through building, finding problem patterns, and learning biblical methods, ask someone. Go to your pastor or that trusted friend. Don't get discouraged. It takes a long time to build a solid building, and we are trying to create something of lasting value.

One beautiful scripture that describes what we are trying to accomplish is Proverbs 24:3 and 4. "Through wisdom is an house builded; and by understanding it is established; and by knowledge shall the chambers be filled with all precious and pleasant riches."

I hope that is your dream! I know it was mine! You will have something beautiful when you're done. Hold on to hope and keep building!

The Architecture of Life

England is a land full of castles! I'll never forget my first visit to Warwick Castle! I could just imagine when it was alive and full of activity instead of tourists!

Did you know castles take hundreds of years to build? And, they are usually built in sections sometimes separated by hundreds of years. Their walls are thick and strong, and their foundations are deep.

That's what we are building, not a straw house for the wolf to blow down! But a protected fortress for God's glory and use. Right? We are working from Proverbs 25:28 – "He that hath no rule over his own spirit is like a city that is broken down, and without walls."

And we need to remind ourselves of 1 Corinthians 3, where the Lord warns us about building our lives with wood, hay, and stubble. We are to be building with gold, silver, and precious stones – building solidly on God's Word.

We are going to do some visualizing today as we talk about castles and walls.

I want you to picture a castle in your mind. It needs to have a drawbridge, some turrets (that's those towers that are in the corners), a middle courtyard, and stone walls. After that, it can be as big or small as you can imagine.

We've spent quite a few visits laying the foundation and learning how to put up the walls, line upon line, precept upon precept, building consistently, right? According to a

Biblical blueprint based on God's promises. So today, for our last visit on depression, we want to look at the other features of our castle.

When you enter a castle, you will sometimes cross the moat and the drawbridge. There is usually either a slabbed inner courtyard or a green parade ground once you get inside. The remainder of the castle is built around this feature. In your mind, I want you to label this courtyard the plain of forgiveness and acceptance.

Underneath this courtyard is forgotten soil. It is the place of silence for the wrongs you have suffered. You now stand on top of those things.

My devotion book, Springs in the Valley, says, "The power to help others depends upon the acceptance of a trampled life." Acceptance – that life is not always what we hope it will be, that things don't always turn out the way we plan, but we are ready to move on, to invite others in, and be the healing balm for them by what they see us building. This forms the flooring for our castle – the parade ground where God's grace can be displayed.

And let's talk about that drawbridge. Not just anyone or anything should be allowed to cross! You need to learn discretion and use wisdom, especially when you are feeling low.

Some people leave their drawbridge open to everything, then wonder why they are overwhelmed. The Bible has lots of instruction here.

2 Cor 6:14 talks about being unequally yoked – the teaching is that we should have fellowship with believers – people with wisdom and like-mindedness who will encourage and build us up. We are to avoid the drama caused by angry people, Proverbs 22:24, foolish people, Proverbs 14:7-9, and even silly people, 2 Timothy 3:6,7. Allowing other people's drama across your drawbridge creates more unnecessary and unhealthy pressure in your life.

So, your drawbridge needs boundaries. You don't have to answer every phone call, text, or message. Sometimes, you just need to turn off that phone, get off the internet, and wait until you are strong enough to deal with what's going on.

And you need to learn to filter things. Don't take offense at everything that is said or everything you hear. Sometimes, people are just talking through their hat or spouting windy words. Let those roll off your back. Use your drawbridge to protect yourself. I'm not talking about shutting yourself away but using wisdom in what you allow into your life. Manage your life by using your drawbridge! You'll be much happier and healthier!

Most every castle has turrets on the corners or in the middle of a long wall. These small towers give strength to the building and define the parameters.

I see them as markers, turning points, places where I was hurt revealing a truth I learned. Turrets do not move. They are part of the architecture of our castle or life.

As people visit your castle, they might ask about the turret, and you can tell them! Zechariah 13:6 says, "And one shall say unto him, what are these wounds in thine hands? Then he shall answer, those with which I was wounded in the house of my friends." This verse is a prophecy about Jesus. Even Jesus had turrets!

These are what I have experienced. They remind me that Jesus was here! They mark where the enemy was defeated, and victory was mine. Wounds can be beautiful – they show that we lived. There is no shame in them, but they cannot be our focus. They are to be used to point others to Christ – to give God glory.

A castle was not just the home of the king or landlord; it was also a place where the villagers would run for safety in case of an invasion. These turrets usually had flags on them and could be seen for miles. Some were low and solid, made for strength, and others were tall and beautiful –to house precious treasures. Some turrets were for battle, hot oil was poured from them onto the attacking enemy.

 Turrets served many purposes, and they can do the same for us. We need turrets of strength – solid places that build our faith, those of beauty and truth – where we house the precious promises of God, and, those that warn the enemy of our preparedness – where we store our shield and armour – where we take a stand for our Lord.

Your life, then, becomes a place of safety for others. Where they can see the beauty of forgiveness, find rest, help, understanding, and encouragement. By standing on your plain of forgiveness, you create a stronger community, and your flags can fly high.

Love is a flag flown high from the castle of my heart for the King is in residence there! Use your castle to point others to Christ and glorify your King.

Then, once the friends are gone, and the sun begins to set, you can walk your castle walls and survey your kingdom. Now you see fruit growing, fertile fields around you, beauty, and even places that need attention, but there is strength to clear new land and reinforce any breeches.

As you see the evening approaching, you'll realize you are no longer a city without walls, but you're productive again, protected, and strong.

We could talk about the dungeon in your castle, where thoughts go to be tried and die.
The armoury where you keep your sword. And even the gatehouse and moat that protects you as an initial defence. But here's the thing. You can't build a while and stop; you need to join the walls fitly together, create that full protection from the enemy, and learn to maintain your castle.

It is my prayer that you will face your depression with God's word and faith in His precious promises and that you will use forgiveness, confession, and the blood of Christ to create sturdy wide walls. That your heart will be open to those in need and ready to share what the battle has taught you with others who need the same hope.

Let's not fix our eyes on our current situation. Let's learn to futurize with Christ. To look beyond today to the tomorrow where we are standing on our wall with His light shining on our faces, and our flags flying high as we say, "He brought me through by His grace alone!"

"Why art thou cast down, O my soul, and why art thou disquieted in me? Hope thou in God: for I shall yet praise him for the help of his countenance." Psalm 42:5